Magnificent Marvelous Me!

This book belongs
to the brilliant and fabulous:

...who is one of a kind and very, very special!

CHILDHAVEN

ART WITH HEART

Welcome to your Book!

Whoever gave you this book must think that you are magnificent AND marvelous! Wow. We are so pleased to meet you! We've got lots of great stuff in store for you… Some of these pages will make you think, others will make you smile, and all of them will help you get to know what's going on inside of you.

Authors usually dedicate their books to special people, and because your artwork is going to be a huge part of making this book wonderful, here's a place for you to dedicate it to whomever you want…

I dedicate this book to _____
because _____

COLOR ME!

Q: How do you make an egg laugh? A: Tell it a yolk.   Q: Why is the sun so bright? A: Because it does its homework!

PENCIL ME IN

HAVE SOME FUN!
Give yourself a moustache! Stick out your tongue! How about an eye patch with earrings that match? Draw 2 eyes or even 3 or just 1 !...

△ Start your nose with a **TRIANGLE**. Try a few on for size.

Is your nose big or small? Is it wide or narrow? Round or pointy?

HEY! WHAT STINKS?

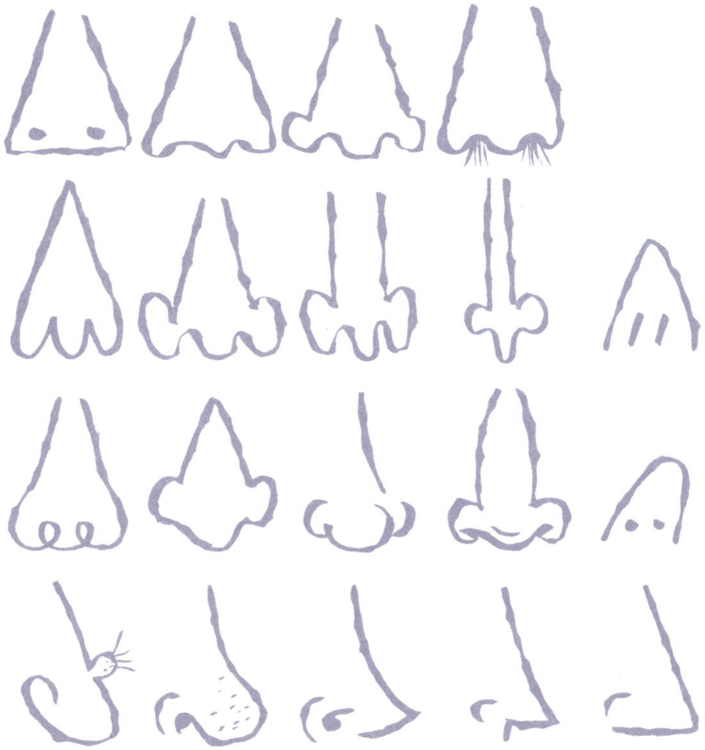

○ Draw two **CIRCLES** or **OVALS** to make eyes.

⌣ Put a **SMILE** on your face with a **SEMI-CIRCLE**.

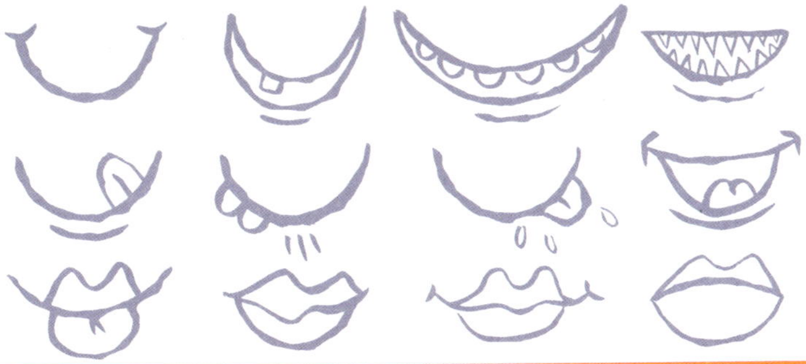

C Pick a **PAIR** of ears.

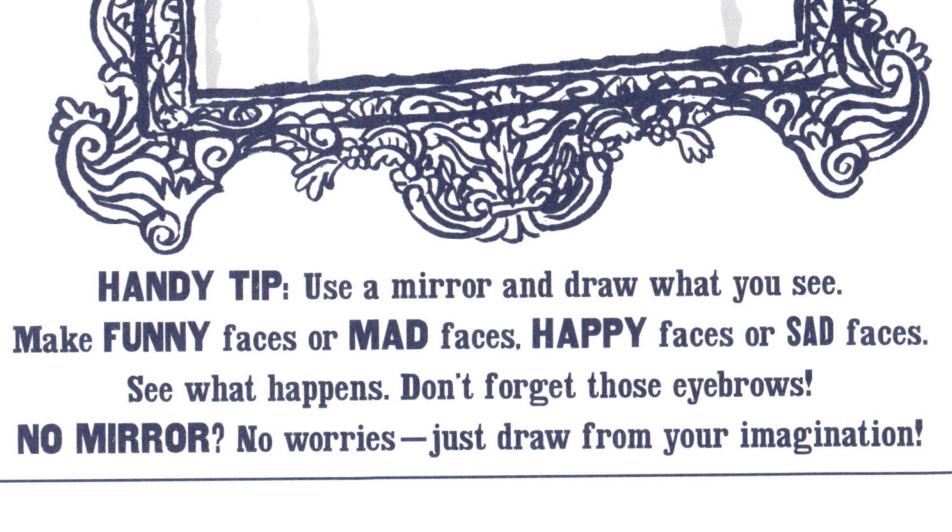

Art is too much fun to be left only to those who are good at it. Elaine Normandy

HANDY TIP: Use a mirror and draw what you see.
Make **FUNNY** faces or **MAD** faces. **HAPPY** faces or **SAD** faces.
See what happens. Don't forget those eyebrows!
NO MIRROR? No worries—just draw from your imagination!

Artwork by MARK KAUFMAN, Seattle, WA

Certificate of Artistic License

THIS IS TO CERTIFY THAT _____ IS HEREBY AUTHORIZED
Your Name Here

BY ART WITH HEART ON THIS ____ DAY OF _____, _____ TO EXERCISE YOUR MAGNIFICENT,
Day *Month* *Year*

ARTISTIC TALENT WITH **COMPLETE** AND **TOTAL** FREEDOM. THIS CERTIFICATE GIVES YOU THE RIGHT

TO EXPERIMENT, DOODLE, IMAGINE, AND CREATE **ANYTIME** YOU ARE INSPIRED TO DO SO.

100%
GUARANTEED AUTHENTIC!

The artist is not a special kind of person; rather each person is a special kind of artist. Ananda Coomaraswamy

THIS LICENSE IS VALID THROUGH THE END OF TIME.

Each of these people is someone who can or has helped you. Write what they do to make you feel better and color them in!

This person helps me by...

Surround yourself with people who will lift you higher. Oprah Winfrey

This person helps me by...

Good works are links that form a chain of love. Mother Teresa

This person helps me by...

Add your own!

Tree of Life

The **roots** of a tree hold up the trunk and help it stand tall. **Leaves** give it food and energy so it can grow. **Flowers** bring extra beauty, which later turn into seeds, helping the process begin again.

On the blossoms, roots, and leaves of this tree, write the names of those who care about you—friends, family, pets, teachers, and organizations…anyone or anything that makes your life better, stronger, or more beautiful.

Many a man with no family tree has succeeded because he branched out for himself. Leo Aikman

Artwork by KEN ORVIDAS, Woodinville, WA

©2008 Art with Heart | artwithheart.org

Artwork by JOHN HASLAM, Bolton, England

Q: What's a sheep's favorite superhero? A: Baa-tman

Q: What is the bad guy's favorite part of any joke? A: The "punch" line!

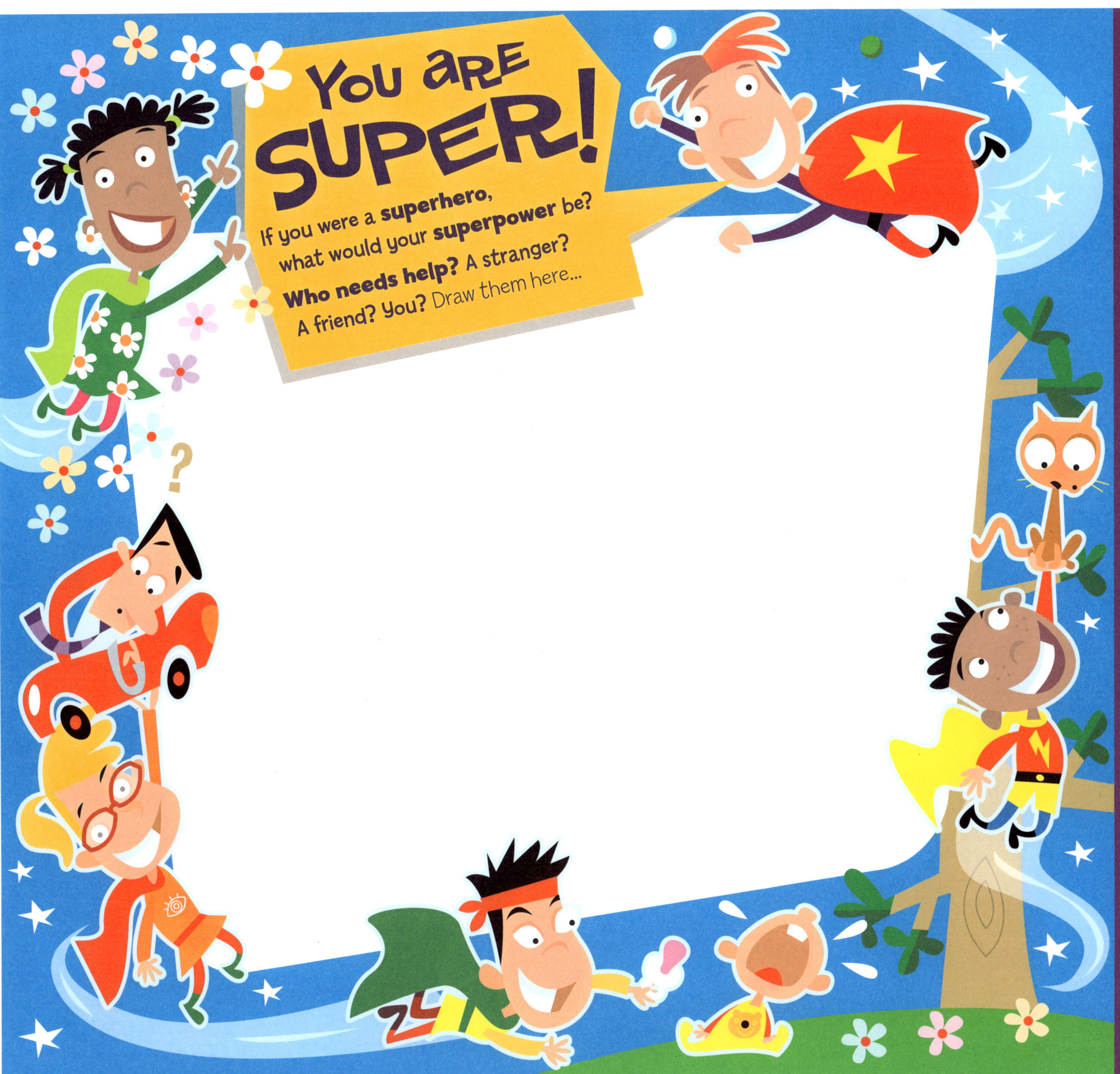

There's No One Like Me in the Whole World!

I am special because I am different! Here are things that make me unique:

This shows my favorite thing to do.

This shows something I'm good at.

This is something very special to me.

No matter what age you are, or what your circumstances might be, you have something unique to offer. Your life, because of who you are, has meaning. — Barbara De Angelis

Artwork by **JULIE PASCHKIS**, Seattle, WA

COLOR ME!

Secret Sauce

good listener, Friendly, Dramatic, Musical, Sweet, artistic, Funny, gentle, Silly, Energetic, Creative, Patient, Playful, Fun, Original, good, smart, happy, kind

This is an unusual recipe for soup. Instead of being made with noodles and veggies, it's made of things that make you a better person...like **courage, strength,** and **kindness**. Use the words on this page to help you figure out what you're made of!

Artwork by **BETSY EVERITT**, London, England

How can you get very far, if you don't know who you are? How can you do what you ought, if you don't know what you've got? *Winnie the Pooh*

©2008 Art with Heart | artwithheart.org

13

LIST THINGS HERE THAT MAKE YOU FEEL SUPER GRUMPY:

LIST THINGS THAT MIGHT HELP YOU FEEL BETTER:

SOMETHING TO THINK ABOUT: What happens when you're grumpy? What do you want to have happen instead?

Worrying is like a rocking chair, it gives you something to do, but it gets you nowhere. Glenn Turner

Problems | Things I Miss | Hard Things

That's the Ticket!

This train is ready to head out. Load up the boxcars with things it's going to take along. Wave goodbye as it leaves the station!

Worries | Wonders | Things I Don't Like

Write more here if you want to…

When you're not feeling great, there are things you can do to help improve your mood. Check what you do to make yourself feel better.

- Hop on a bike
- Make a fort
- Talk to someone
- Tell a joke
- Have a snack
- Swing on a swing!
- Listen to music
- Spend time with friends
- Dance!
- Read a book
- Color
- Help someone else
- Jump rope!
- Pat a pet
- Go outside

Draw other things you like to do...

Artwork by **DANIELLE JONES**, Toronto, Canada

Q: Why didn't the car feel well? A: Because it had gas! Q: Why was the cookie sad? A: Because it felt crummy!

©2008 Art with Heart | artwithheart.org

17

Sweet Talk

In this game, each person takes turns and flips a penny onto the page. Wherever the coin lands, the player asks that question to the person sitting to their right. If the coin touches more than one question, you choose which one they should answer. If it lands on "Free Choice," you can ask any question you want to. Ready? Set? Go!

- Describe a time when you were proud of yourself.
- What's your favorite thing to eat in the entire world?
- What 5 words would your best friend use to describe you?
- What's an important thing for people to know about you?
- What do people ask you that annoys you?
- Snort like a pig!
- What's your favorite smell?
- Give a compliment.
- Where's your favorite place to be and why do you like it?
- Use 3 words to describe how you feel right now.
- Talk about a happy memory.
- If you had 3 wishes, what would you wish for?
- If you could meet anyone, who would it be? Why?
- What makes you feel sad?
- If you could change one thing about the place you live, what would it be?
- Free Choice
- If you could be invisible, what would you do?
- What do you like about school? What don't you like?
- How do you show someone that they are special?
- What makes you feel happy?
- What are you really good at? What do you want to get better at?
- What makes you the very happiest?
- Make a silly face!
- Talk about when you did a good deed and how it made you feel.
- Lose a turn!
- If you were an animal, which one would you be? Why?
- What do you want to be when you grow up?
- Get a compliment!
- What's your favorite dream?
- Talk about a time when you felt super smart.
- If you could change the world, what would you do?
- Finish this sentence: "I feel _____ when you _____. I'd like to feel _____ instead."
- What do you want to get better at? Why?
- Get up & dance!
- Talk about a time you got into trouble.
- What makes you feel jealous?

Artwork by ANNE BRYANT, Seattle, WA

FACE IT!

Which one of these animals looks sad to you? Happy? Angry? Lonely? Why do you think they feel that way? Color them in and label their feelings.

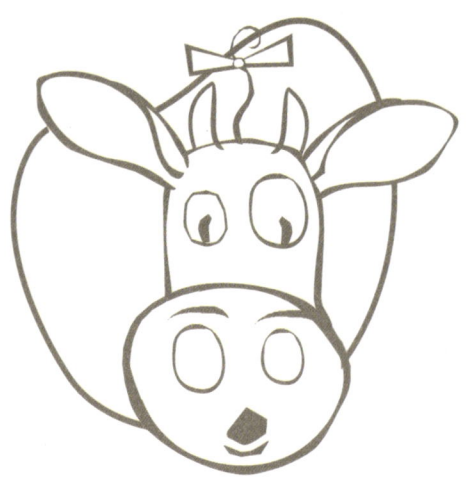

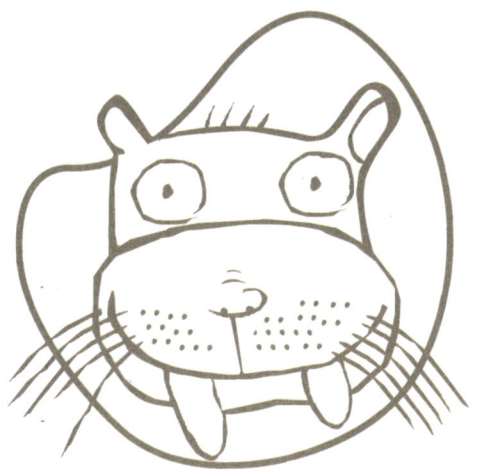

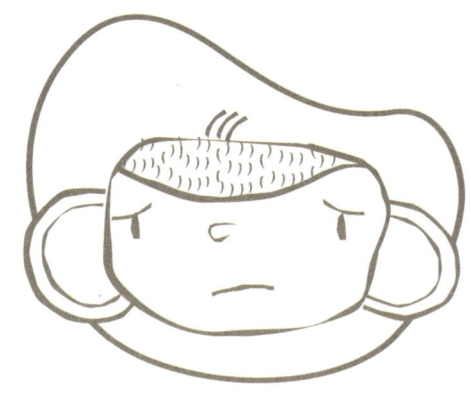

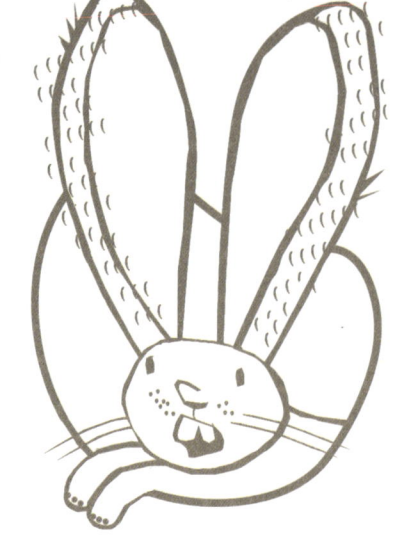

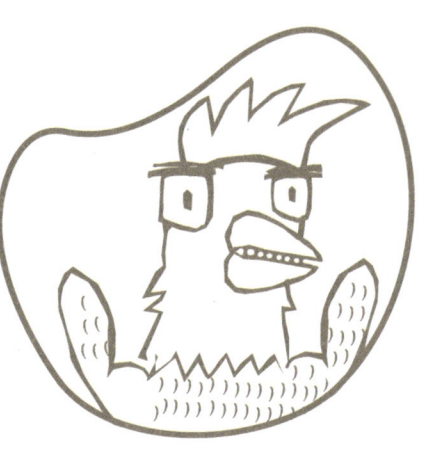

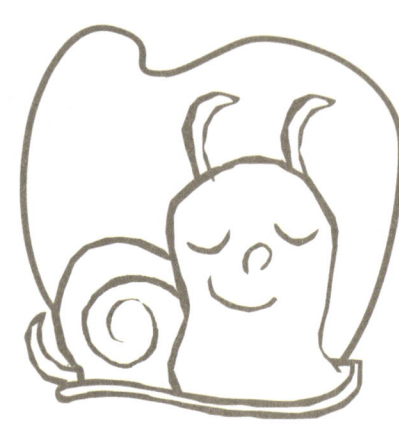

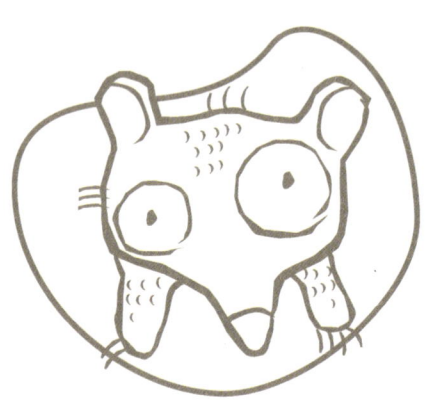

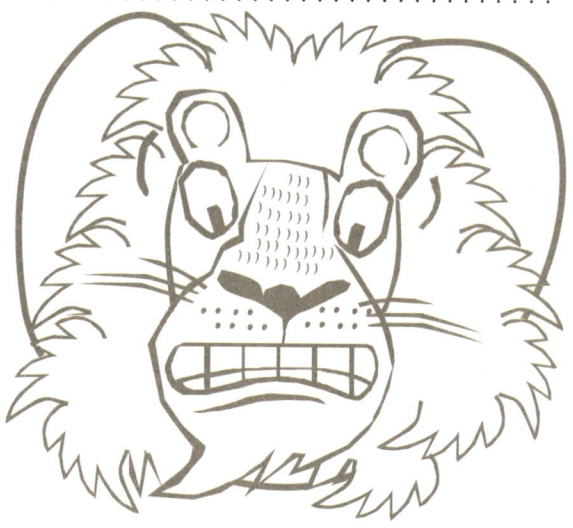

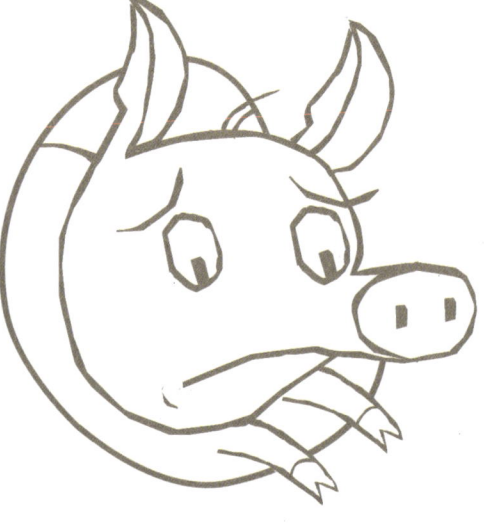

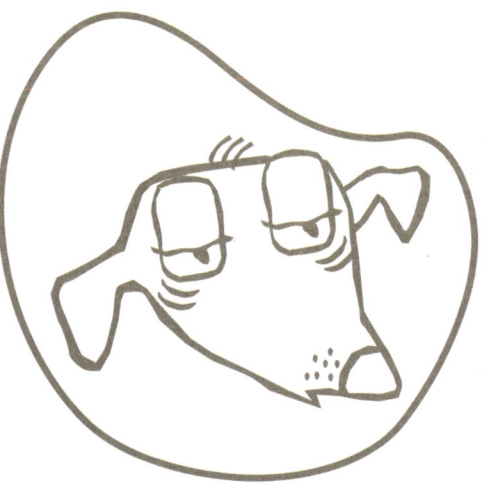

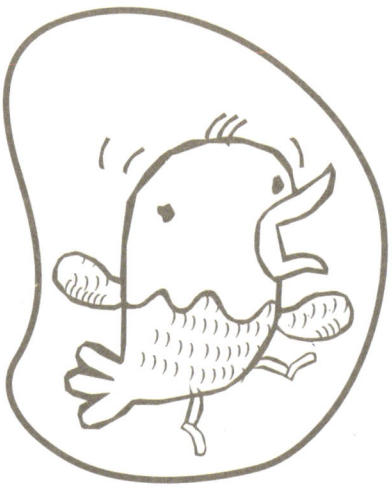

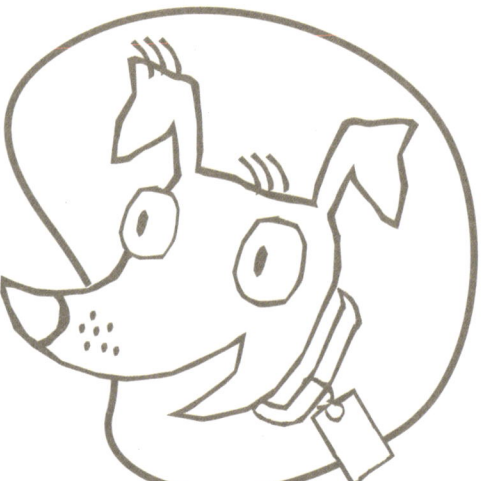

Q: What do cows like to dance to? A: Country moo-sic!

Q: What do you call a pig that knows karate? A: Pork chop!

Artwork by **AMANDA SHEPHERD**, Phoenix, AZ

DRAW SOMETHING THAT SHOWS WHAT LIFE LOOKED LIKE WHEN YOU WERE YOUNGER...

DRAW WHAT YOUR LIFE LOOKS LIKE TODAY...

DRAW WHAT YOUR LIFE MIGHT LOOK LIKE IN A WEEK...OR A YEAR.

Q: What do you get when you cross a parrot with a centipede? A: A walkie-talkie

Q: Why do hummingbirds hum? A: Because they don't know the words.

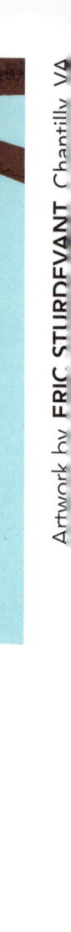

Artwork by ERIC STURDEVANT Chantilly VA

©2008 Art with Heart | artwithheart.org

22

Sometimes people have special things that help them

...like glasses help people see and wheelchairs help people move around more easily. What's helpful to people you know? Why are these things important? How do they help?

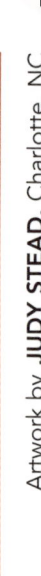

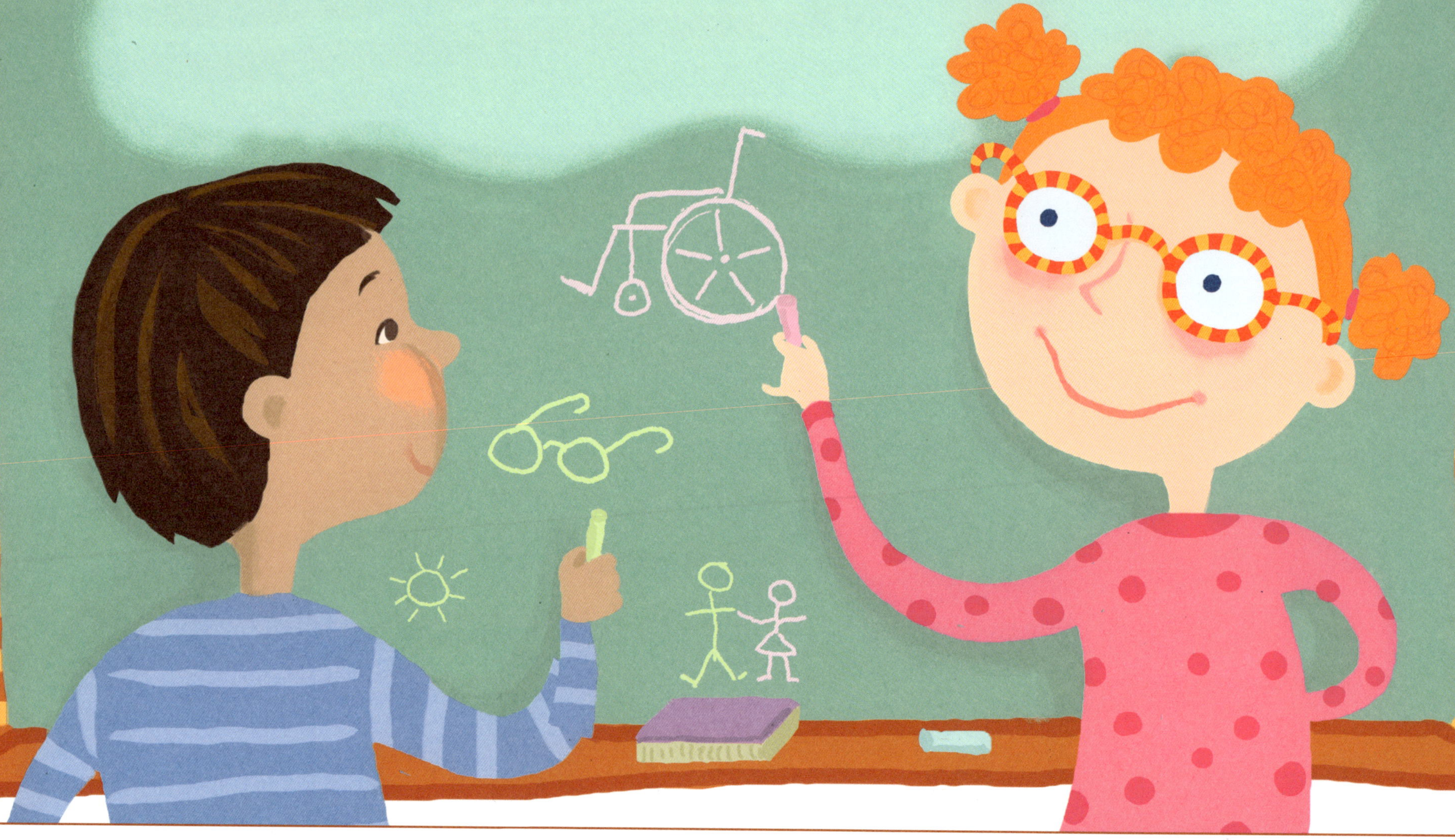

Q: Why shouldn't you tell a joke to a block of ice? A: It will crack up!

Q: What do you get when you peel two bananas? A: A pair of slippers!

Artwork by JUDY STEAD, Charlotte, NC

FEELINGS MASKS

Some feelings are easier to show than others. On the first mask, draw the face that you show to others. On the second mask, draw a face that shows the feelings that you sometimes keep private.

With every experience, you alone are painting your own canvas, thought by thought, choice by choice. *Oprah Winfrey*

Artwork by **HARVEY CHAN**, Toronto, Canada

©2008 Art with Heart | artwithheart.org

Emotion Ocean

From far away, the ocean can look calm. But once you are in it, you may find that the waves are strong enough to push you around...

Draw what makes the water rough and scary. Then draw what you need to stay safe. What can make you stronger and help you through the storm?

Artwork by **CHRISTIANE BEAUREGARD**, Montréal, Canada

Q: Why did the starfish cross the ocean? A: To get to the other tide!

Q: Why don't oysters donate to charity? A: Because they're shellfish.

©2008 Art with Heart | artwithheart.org

We all have things we worry about.

In Guatemala, when a child can't sleep because they are worried, they are given special dolls to tell their troubles to. Tell these "worry dolls" what's on your mind…

"Courage doesn't always roar. Sometimes courage is the quiet voice at the end of the day saying, 'I will try again tomorrow.'" *Anonymous*

Today, I was thinking about you and wondering if you were:
❏ baking cookies   ❏ doing my homework for me   ❏ doing well.

Yesterday, I turned the corner and saw:
❏ the principal buying polka dotted underwear
❏ someone who reminded me of you
❏ ....

When I think about you, I:
❏ wiggle like a worm and giggle like a hyena
❏ can't help but smile from ear to ear!
❏ ....

When I see you next, I will:
❏ put a wacky wig on   ❏ ....
❏ pretend I'm a chicken   ....
❏ give you a huge hug   ....

And one more thing: ....
....
....

Draw your picture here and autograph it!

Dear ....

....
....
....
....
....
....
....

❏ Signed ❏ Love ❏ Hugs ❏ Later Tater ❏ ....

❏ Your Friend ❏ The Best Kid in the World ❏ ....

.... (sign it here)

Draw your picture here and autograph it!

40

Food for Thought!

Do you ever feel sad, sluggish, or hyper without knowing why?

Did you know that what you eat affects how you feel?

Your body is like a car — it needs good fuel to keep on going!

Draw some unhealthy and healthy food below.

Q: Why do donuts go to the dentist? A: To get fillings!   Q: Why do French people eat snails? A: Because they don't like fast food!

HA HA! HEE HEE! HO HO!

This is the funniest thing that ever happened to me:

This is my favorite joke or riddle:

Artwork by **SEYMOUR CHWAST**, New York, NY

Here are some jokes to share!

What weighs 5,000 pounds and wears glass slippers? Cinderelephant

What did one volcano say to the other volcano? I lava you!

What does the gingerbread boy put on his bed? A cookie sheet.

Why did the clown put his cake in the freezer? He wanted icing on it!

Why won't sharks eat clowns? Because they taste funny!

How do you make a Kleenex dance? Put a little boogie in it!

Why did the ocean roar? You would too if you had crabs on your bottom!

Knock, Knock! Who's there?

Tank! Tank who? You're welcome!

Howl! Howl Who? Howl you know unless you open the door?

Old lady! Old lady, who? Wow! I didn't know you could yodel!

Anita! Anita who? Anita to borrow a dollar!

Police! Police who? Police stop telling these awful knock-knock jokes!

What did the porcupines say after they hugged? Ouch!

What word is always spelled incorrectly? Incorrectly!

Q: What did the Summer say to the Spring? A: Help! I'm going to Fall!

Q: Why was Six afraid of Seven? A: Because Seven Eight (ate) Nine!

©2008 Art with Heart | artwithheart.org

43

BEST DAY EVER!

It's your choice — what would you like to do today? Where will you go? Who will you bring with you? Draw it here…

Yesterday is history. Tomorrow is a mystery. And today is a gift. That's why we call it the present. Babatunde Olatunji

The Magnificent Artists
These artists donated their time & talent especially for YOU!

Because **GABRIELE ANTONINI** can't fly, he wishes he had a friend (like a bat or an eagle) who could. Much of the artwork he creates is for children's books. He is happy to be a part of this project because he knows that lots of small contributions add up to make big and wonderful things that help many. (pg. 36)

One of **MARK ATHERTON'S** earliest memories is of sitting in front of a huge pile of paper, just happily drawing all day long. Fortunately, he still gets to do that now that he's all grown up. Being creative makes him happier than anything else in the world and he hopes these pages will inspire you to discover how marvelous making art can be. (pg. 18)

As a boy, **KREIG BARRIE** whiled away the hours drawing robots and spaceships. Forty-some years later, he draws pictures for a living on a super-fast computer that's so smart it can beat him in chess AND calculate how many gallons of ice cream could fill the Grand Canyon. He lives near the Washington coast and regularly has herds of elk pass through his back yard. (pg. 46)

MARTY BAUMANN enjoys frozen yogurt and collects old comic books. He loves dogs and playing blues guitar. He hopes that you remember that every kind thing you do helps make the universe a better place to live for everyone. (pg. 24)

CHRISTIANE BEAUREGARD makes great homemade French fries—and speaks fluent French! When things get rough, she listens to that small inner voice to help keep her on track. She did a page in here as a way of showing gratitude for what she's been given. (pg. 33)

Some of **RUSSELL BENFANTI's** best memories are of when he and his four brothers and sister made forts in the family room. He believes that if we never have bad days, we can't appreciate the good ones. You might recognize his style because he has done art for Walt Disney, Fisher-Price, Hasbro, LeapFrog, Milton Bradley, and more! (pg. 27)

BRIAN BIGGS is an illustrator and animator as well as a ukulele and accordion player. His career in children's books began with the *Shredderman* series and he has since illustrated lots of other books too. He enjoys playing with his kids, who are more fun than and dancing monkeys! (pg. 8)

KRISTINE BROGNO is the Art Director for Children's Books at Chronicle Books. She and her two sons collect bottle caps and other fun items to make art with. She comes from a big, loud Italian family: she has 6 siblings and 13 nieces and nephews so far. She believes that art—in any form—makes life better. (pg. 37)

ANNE BRYANT grew up in Ohio, where she and her brother made snow horses. They'd feed them carrots and imagine galloping down the frosty path. When she's not being creative, she practices her pet whispering technique on her kitties. She has a sweet tooth and collects antique buttons. (pg. 19)

Even though **HARVEY CHAN** was born in Hong Kong, he knows that you and he are very similar. He also knows that it's really important to talk to someone you trust when you're feeling down. He now lives in Canada and always gives 200% to his projects: 100% for his client, and 100% for himself. (pg. 32)

As the co-founder of Push Pin Studios, **SEYMOUR CHWAST's** designs and illustrations have been used in ads, animated films, and lots of children's books. The Museum of Modern Art, and even the Israel Museum in Jerusalem, have his posters. He was an only child and spent a large part of his time blissfully drawing away. (pg. 43)

MIKE DAMMER spent a lot of time camping with his brothers and sisters as a kid. He still loves being outside, but now enjoys being inside too. He collects old things like barber chairs, pay phones, and parking meters. If he could talk to you, he would encourage you to find something that you really enjoy doing and spend a lot of time getting good at it—or at least have the most fun you can! (pg. 6)

HELEN DARDIK'S favorite foods are olives and watermelons. She likes shopping with her sister and playing video games with her brother. If she wasn't an artist, she'd be an opera singer or a fashion designer. (pg. 29)

LINDA DAVICK is always getting into trouble because of the tricks she plays (but her friends forgive her anyway). She is kind to herself by loving even the funny-looking bits, getting enough sleep, and not getting angry with herself—even when it's hard to understand how to do something. (pg. 9)

NANCY DAVIS enjoys collecting tin toys, ironstone china, bird cages, and seashells. She is equally comfortable drawing as she is needle-pointing. Some of her children's books include *A Garden of Opposites* and *Flicker Flash*. (pg. 42)

BETSY EVERITT and her three brothers cooled down during hot summers by riding bikes and eating popsicles. Because making art can feel isolating at times, she's thrilled to have joined a lot of caring artists whose love for children has inspired them to donate their work to this book. She uses gouache on watercolor paper for her illustrations. (pg. 13)

All **DOUG FRASER** really wants to do is make art and ride a motorcycle under sunny skies. He is best known for his work for NIKE, the National Hockey League (NHL), and Suzuki Motorcycles. He has a Master's Degree from the School of Visual Arts in New York City, and lives in British Columbia, Canada. (pg. 10)

DANIEL GUIDERA grew up in Brooklyn way back when dinosaurs ruled the earth. His favorite things were black-and-white flying saucer movies, stickball, and baseball cards. His art education started with Saturday morning cartoons and comic books. And, if he had words of wisdom to share, they would be (paraphrasing from his favorite pro wrestler), "Just when they think they have all the answers, change the questions!" (pg. 44)

If **JOHN HASLAM** was a superhero, he would do all his work while asleep and spend his awake hours thinking up silly ideas to make the world laugh. As a child, he enjoyed digging in the garden. Now that he's grown up, he can't imagine being anything but an artist! (pg. 11)

LYDIA HESS was 11 when her brother was born. When he was older, they'd take walks in the woods or go rowing on the lake. She made sure to include him in things because she wanted him to know that he could count on his sister. She creates a lot of her art on scratchboard. (pg. 34)

JESSICA HISCHE collects dresses and enjoys hearty meals, celebrity news, her friends, and vintage type. She works from her apartment at a desk covered with half-filled cups of coffee, candy wrappers, and random knickknacks. She found children's picture books to be quite inspiring while growing up and hopes that you will be inspired by her work too! (pg. 39)

When **DANIELLE JONES** was five, she really wanted a dog, but was allergic. Instead, she got a Lucky Troll doll with orange hair. She still has it. One of the things she's learned is that sometimes the best way to help yourself through a rough time is to help someone else. Kellogg's, Baskin-Robbins, and Milton Bradley have all hired her for her artistic skills. (pg. 17)

When **MARK KAUFMAN** was nine, he sent an application to NASA to become an astronaut. When he discovered that he had to be really good at math and science to become one, he decided he'd rather draw and stay firmly planted here on earth where he can use his powers for good and not evil. (pg. 3)

NORA KRUGG isn't a picky eater...she loves almost anything! Once, when she and her siblings went to the zoo, her favorite stuffed animal fell into the bear's cage. Luckily, the bear was a picky eater too and left it alone. Her work has appeared on both Comedy Central and MTV. She moved from Germany to teach illustration at Parson's School of Design in New York. (pg. 15)

RICH LILLASH has three sisters and a brother. His grandmother used to do art projects with them, which is where he got his start. Now, he enjoys doing art with his 3 daughters. He thinks that doing art is a great way to get your mind off sad or difficult times. His artwork has won awards and his clients include lots of magazines that grown-ups read. (48+this page)

STEFFANIE LORIG loves to write. She and her husband wrote a book called *Such a Silly Baby*, while tickling their son. She has written seven other books too for Art with Heart and she even wrote a book for young baseball fans. She grew up super shy, but through art and writing, she found her voice along with what she wanted to say. She is the founder of Art with Heart, a nonprofit that helps kids. She hopes you like this book and that you'll write to tell her what you thought about it! (pg. 38)